Collection of Hidden Thoughts

Amalija Glavan

BookLeaf Publishing

India | USA | UK

Presentation by *BookLeaf Publishing*

Web: www.bookleafpub.com

E-mail: info@bookleafpub.com

ISBN: 9789358313154

First edition 2024

DEDICATION

To everyone who supported me and inspired me to keep writing.

PREFACE

Poetry is not liked by everyone. However, it doesn't exist to be liked or disliked. It is a form of art. It exists to speak its language and convey a message. Whether you understand it, accept it, refuse it, or ignore it, is up to you. Whether you like it or appreciate it, is up to you. Whether you take it forward, is up to you. I am merely a messenger, and this book is my message. Thank you for taking the time to read it. I hope some of its words speak to you.

Stranger

Sitting on the bench, staring at the sea,
book in his arms, mole like a pea.
Still as a statue while people walk by,
sometimes it looks like he is going to cry.

Always there, but easy to miss,
breathing the air, somehow amiss.
Reaches his bag while taking a sip,
there is a slight tremble in his lip.

He stands to go, but looks away,
no step is made, he wants to stay.
He pulls his glasses to the tip of the nose,
the feeling he has for this place is close.

He walks away, head held low,
however still, it makes him glow.
I feel the cold as the wind starts to blow,
what his thoughts were, I might never know.

Flowers in a vase

Every day, as I walk by,
I can see the reflection of the sky
on that window down the road,
while I let my mind unload.

Every day, as I look in,
I can see a glimpse of within
the room filled with nothing but books,
and the back wall with two old hooks.

Every day, as I walk away,
I can see the same pot of clay
carrying the big glass vase,
in it two flowers with red face.

Every day, as I look back,
I can see a lady in black
sitting on the side of the house,
sewing the button onto the blouse.

Every day, as I cross the street,
I enter the cafe and I take a seat.
I close my eyes and there they are,
those two flowers looking from afar.

Every day, as I take my tea,
how easy it would be, I see,
to forget about the beauty of that place
in this world without any grace.

Every day, as I stand up to leave,
I think of it and start to believe
all the caring those flowers get,
just to make a beautiful set,
will once be gone and no one will know
how those flowers can make you glow.

Trapped

Rain pouring down, so thick you could hardly
see,
wind blowing strong, the trees trying to break
free…
And she just sat there.

Leaves twirling around until they land, all wet,
and stay all over her, they stick there, they set…
And she just sat there.

All the flowers that once proudly stood,
now battered down with rage, gone for good…
And she just sat there.

Grass lively green, just freshly cut,
has now gone brown, all turned to mud…
And she just sat there.

Birds in a tree, tight together in the nest,
trying to hide and stay dry, chest to chest…
And she just sat there.

The smell of air is crisp, cuts deep to the bone,
it is wet and dry; it sits like a stone…
And she just sat there.

She never moves, she makes no sound,
her limbs are free, but they still seem bound.
And she just sat there…

…because she shouldn't go where she could,
and she couldn't go where she should.

Captured

Hair golden like rays of sunshine,
skin pale like porcelain.
Lips red like the poppy fields,
smile enchanting, yet very thin.

The way colours align makes you feel elated,
the way lines entwine makes you feel alive.
The way it feels to touch makes you feel
positive,
the way it breathes the air makes you want to
thrive.

The sky behind is drowning blue,
the cherry tree floats in bloom.
The fields filled with hay, true.

The way the view angles makes you reach out
for the clouds.
The way patters emerge makes you run your
fingers through blooms.
The way it spins the world makes you never
want to see the crowds.

The grass still has the drops of dew,
the path is full of dust and mud.

The way the markings twist makes you wonder
if there is a cue.
The way it captures the attention makes you
escape while staying put.

However, you are completely bound,

because it is only a picture you have found.

The beauty in the flower

Golden is the aura around it,
and sparkling is the way it moves,
when the wind comes with its chilly hands
and gently pushes the small grooves.

Every time the moves differ from the last,
as it swings to the nature of music the air plays.
It bows to the ground or it stands still,
either way, the dance goes on while it stays.

The rain has started and it made it hard
for the little body to weight it out,
but along comes the stronger wind
and once again, the dance wins over clout.

Despite all the battering down,
despite all the blowing away,
despite all the natures ways,
it stands there and continues to sway.

The feeble among the strong

Looking at the bare walls, searching for a
difference in the texture.
Looking at broken windows, searching for
patterns to emerge.
Looking at battered doors, searching for signs of
aged wood.

And it still stands.

Looking at the scattered leaves on the floor, dry
and brittle.
Looking at the grains of dust on the shelves,
white and dense.
Looking at the ants in the corner, fast and busy.

And it still stands.

Looking at the ceiling, partly collapsed and still
falling.
Looking at the floor, boards all broken and still
dying.
Looking at the old wardrobe, doors ajar and
transparent.

And it still stands.

Looking at the stairway, no carpet left to spare.
Looking at the lamps, the shades eaten away.
Looking at the shoes, the soles rotten and smell.

And it still stands.

Outside the world has changed and the buildings
stand tall.
Outside the grounds are kept and the plants
encouraged to grow.
Outside the air is crisp and the life is felt in the
breeze.

But it still stands.

It has been years since he has gone without
return.
It has been years he told them it will never be
the same.
It has been years since anyone has remembered.

But it still stands.

A stool in a barn

Just a fragile farm in the middle of nowhere.
Just a place of quiet and calm.
Just a place of beautiful mornings and stunning
evenings.
Just a place of infinite joy.

Endless fields surround the house, endless trees
guard its lines.
Endless plants wherever you look, endless birds
to sing a song.

You look up, you see the sky just as it is, no
mask or hide.
You close your eyes, you hear the sounds of
nature, no noise.
You inhale and it is crisp and fresh, no poison to
clog your pipe.

The house on a small hill, in the middle of it all.
The best place for detaching from the world,
the best place for thinking out loud,
the best place for changing your life.

There is a barn at the back, in the valley, next to
stream.

Small and feeble, with stone in green mould.
It stands strong despite the times; rains give it a
glow.
It is empty inside, all but a small stool.

I look at it and it makes me think how it affected
her mind, how it made her tick.
I fail to understand how a place like this can
make a person do what she did.

It makes no sense, in this place, in this calm.

Everyone thought she came here to heal, yet this
place sems to have made it worse.
For her to end her life in this barn, with only a
stool and that ground glass.

This just goes to prove that all the calmness in
the world
cannot help when there are screams of despair
within your mind and soul.

Struggle

The sky was cloudy yet again, storm on the way.
The dark was falling quick, less time to play.
Sounds died out, the roads became quiet,
yet there was no time to admit to getting tired.

So soft and smooth, like silk it was,
nobody can forget the way it awes.
As the light escaped the day,
the white of silk has turned to grey.

Soft, so quiet, the time has come,
yet somehow the approach was loud.
With each second it was more numb
and the only star was covered by cloud.

At first the pain was pulsing, and it was cold,
there was no other way than to fold.
What was once red has become blue,
and what were lies has become true.

The strength that was always there
was fierce at first, but now is bare.
The silence that was once a blessing
has become harder than confessing.

It turned the youth inside out,
it bound within all that clout.
The green sparkle once so alive
was now only trying to survive.

At times it took long, at times it was a blink.
Either way, there was the stink
that no amount of water can cure,
and nothing can again make it pure.

When the light starts breaking again,
trying to pry into the small den,
it closes up, its curtains drawn,
fearing how quick again it will be gone.

Sometimes is easier

Sun is shining, the skies are clear,
the shadows are gold, the warmth is near.
You can smell the crisp air
of spring fighting winter in despair.

But even in the brightest of days
the storm can come and bring the greys.
The rain will pour and batter down,
and turn the world into mud brown.

One drop will fall on the hair, long and dry,
one will touch the cheek, red and shy.
One slid by the eye, naturally blue,
one wet the brow, looking for a clue.

The one on the shoulder slid down to nail,
another on stomach with no avail.
While some sprinkle down the bottom
thinking they are already in autumn.

Some go down the legs and knees
stinging like a swarm of bees,
while shaking down the rest
that seem to think they are the best.

More then come and start again,
using you like a rusted drain,
clearing out all the spots
and tying all the stronger knots.

They might be drops but like stones they feel
when they are dropped while you kneel.
Even wet they will burn,
no matter how many times you turn.

All you know to do when they hit
is to walk away and simply quit.
Might not be the answer you were looking for
but it is the only one that keeps you ashore.

Just because

They bring you clothes, but they never fit.
Sometimes they're too small, sometimes too big.
Most of the time they are already worn,
and all the time they smell of corn.

They bring you food, but it is always cold.
Sometimes it is canned, sometimes it grew
mould.
Most of the time it is past the date
and all the time in the same crate.

They bring you drink, but it is never full.
Sometimes in bottles, sometimes a spoonful.
Most of the time it is leftover of bad taste
and all the time it is not a waste.

They bring you paper, but it is always old.
Sometimes they miss pages, sometimes they
fold.
Most of the time they tell of hardship
and all the time they feel like a whip.

They bring you things so they feel in power,
sometimes it works, sometimes it's just dour.
Most of the time it stays the same

and all the time they claim the fame.

Why

When she speaks up, she gets ignored,
If she doesn't get laughed at.

Why?

When she asks a question, she gets ignored,
If she doesn't get laughed at.

Why?

When she offers help, she gets ignored,
If she doesn't get laughed at.

Why?

When she wears her best clothes, she gets
ignored,
If she doesn't get laughed at.

Why?

When she chases her dreams, she gets ignored,
If she doesn't get laughed at.

Why?

When she accomplishes something, she gets ignored,
If she doesn't get laughed at.

Why?

When she is being her true self, she gets ignored,
If she doesn't get laughed at.

Why?

When she stands up for herself, she gets ignored,
If she doesn't get laughed at.

Why?

Because she didn't decide, it was decided for her.

The old man and the grit

Every morning, together with dawn,
you could see him walk down the street,
in the long jumper that was hand knit,
and his tools wrapped in an old sheet.

Every morning, as the light broke,
he walked slowly, with a stride,
the aura around him refused to abide,
nobody could make his world collide.

Every morning, as the first rays shone,
he put his hand up, shielding his eyes,
pushing forward, refusing to compromise
with what everyone says his age implies.

Every morning, even when it rained,
you could spot him in his plastic coat,
swimming through the street with a gloat,
just to reach the harbour and his boat.

Every morning, no matter the wind,
his wrinkly hands shaking with cold,
he would never give in or fold,
he would never let himself feel old.

Later in the day, he would walk back,
probably tired, but always with a smile.
He has fixed another fault of crack
and handled the net so gentile.

One day he didn't show,
there were no tools, the walk that was slow.
One day, it was so strange,
he didn't show and I knew there was a change.

Later that week I saw he was gone,
and since that day, it changed the tone.
Now I wake up and watch at dawn,
just a boat, sea and a seagull alone.

Quick to glide

Eyes so dark, with depths uncovered,
feathers so bright, with colours to be discovered.

Beak so sharp, with power unknown,
clutches so strong, with eagerness for the throne.

Song so loud, with tones in the heights,
sound so quiet, with fire it ignites.

Wings so long, with wind they fight,
head held high, with feelings of delight.

Flying so high, no limit in sight,
believing yourself, feeling no fright.

Yet one little blink is enough
for the world to turn tough,
and you are no longer in control,
you end up paying the toll.

One word

One word is enough
to take the money of the helpless person.

One word is enough
to turn the person away from help.

One word is enough
to take the home away from a poor person.

One word is enough
to turn the person against another one.

One word is enough
to take the courage away from a shy person.

One word is enough
to turn the happy moment into a sad one.

One word is enough
to take the fear and use it to gain power.

One word is enough
to turn the child away from pursuing the dream.

One word is enough

to take the power away from a person.

One word is enough
to turn a second of joy into lifetime of horror.

One word is enough
to take the ability to support oneself away.

One word is enough
to turn the person away from a good deed.

One word is enough
to take the hope away from someone.

How come one word is not enough
to stop all that?

Mask

Looking at herself in the mirror
she tries to decide what makes her look cheerer.
Which tools to reach for today
so she doesn't have to use words to say.

She picks up the brush and looks at the palette,
it weights in her hand like a mallet.
She looks at the mirror once more
and pulls up the bottle from the drawer.

Darker foundation must be applied,
she puts it on with a known stride,
using a known circular motion
Trying to cover up an ocean.

She uses the darker eyeshadow,
a few shades of blue applied slow.
Using the tapping of the brush
to pace herself, not to rush.

She picks up the dark red lipstick,
opening it up with that same click.
A shade so dark it looks like blood
to cover up the underneath mud.

With a shaking hand she takes the blush,
applies it thinly with her big brush,
but as she is looking at her face
she starts to pick up the pace.

She puts the make up on every day
to cover the fact her life is more than grey.
She doesn't know how to ask for help,
so she hopes this way she stays herself.

Antique patterns

She is being taught to be quiet and sweet,
while he is being taught to always take the
heath.

They read her the stories where a princess
always needs saving,
while he hears about the strong warriors and
their braving.

She is being taught how to appear dutiful,
while he is being taught to choose only
beautiful.

They tell her she needs to know how to behave,
while they tell him it is his right to always crave.

She has to choose a career to suit her role as a
wife,
while he can choose a career to suit him for life.

They tell her she has to always show emotion,
while they tell him to stay strong and bury them
in an ocean.

She is groomed to be a mother from the first toy,

while he gets to learn how to be a real boy.

Why can't they just choose what they want to
be,
why do we limit the world they should see?

Why can't they learn at their own pace,
why do we have to limit their space?

Why can't they feel what they actually feel,
why do we push for what we think is real?

Why is society so frightened
to allow their youngsters to be enlightened?

Scene

They see tattoos all over your arms,
they become vary, it rings all sorts of alarms.

They see your shoes, all platform and leather,
they say nothing, but it changes the weather.

They see your hair, up in a pink spike,
they cross the street, take a hike.

They see your shirt, wrinkled and shaded,
they hide a smile, consider you downgraded.

They see your trousers, not ironed and bright,
They turn away, you don't get an invite.

They see your jacket, torn at the side,
they feel endangered and want to hide.

What they miss to see is the way you walk,
the confidence behind it, the way you talk.

What they miss to hear are your words,
the brains behind it, like song of birds.

What they miss to feel is the warm,

the strength you have to fight through the storm.

Why is the appearance always the key
to how we proceed, to how we agree?

Why is it that in this day and age,
the whole world is like an ancient stage?

Winter's night

Frost on the windows as you look outside,
fox trying to find a place to hide.
There is not a soul inside
that doesn't want that special ride.

Some are hoping for the snow to fall,
while others are decorating a tree in the hall.
The peace and quiet, like there is a wall
that blocks the evil once and for all.

On some days stars are bright,
while on others clouds are airtight.
Peering through the door, waiting to bite
that special homemade winter delight.

That special smell that comes from cold
and somehow gathers your breath to behold.
Whoever breathes it, young or old,
feels nothing can ever make them fold.

As nights are getting longer
And the cold growing stronger,
you see the Winter in all its glory
and you are in the middle of its story.

Summer's eve

Porch that looks out to the sea,
a splash of pinot, a taste of brie,
some raw olives for a special glee,
and a breeze of wind to set you free.

Days are long, night takes time
like it is running away from crime.
The smell of the freshly cut lime
brings back the memories prime.

The tree of figs so big and sweet,
always better than any other treat.
Walking around on bare feet,
never feeling the boiling heat.

The feelings always buried deep
while trying to drift off, to sleep.
The life might have looked cheap
but it was only ours to keep.

The pain digs in, claws at the soul,
trying to dig up the old coal.
Summers were our lives best days,
we were in control of the ending of plays.

Spring morning

The light finds its way out earlier now,
in front of the long night it doesn't bow.
More warmth it wants to allow
for the nature to wake up somehow.

A bird sings, that is the first sound,
the type of song that wakes up the ground.
The first signs of life break through, bound
to find a way into the world, so profound.

The breath taken in, it starts to smell,
the kind of fragrance that will always dwell.
The power it has to make the nature rebel
as it casts its spirits around like a spell.

A look around, being able to see,
how the nature seems to agree
it is time to come up and break free
in search for fresh food, a flower for a bee.

At first, it might feel as too much
when the Spring brings in its touch.
However, it brings the life out of the doom
and in short time makes it resume.

Autumn's day

What was once green, now turned yellow,
the shades of brown coming, never mellow.
Coming slowly, that one faithful fellow
playing its string on a natural cello.

There is no palette greater this
which can turn any change into bliss.
If you let it work its power, let it kiss,
it will make a new life out of the abyss.

There is a crisp change in the air,
like a fine curtain it might tear.
Fine movements, found so rare,
never seemed to need a spare.

Weather changes, here comes the rain,
slow at first, then fills up the drain.
Never the one to cause any pain,
yet blamed as one to put up a chain.

Autumn is the most famous painter,
the talent is all there, without a trainer.
It all comes so quiet, lower than a whisper,
as the day get shorter and the feeling crisper.